Grow Up

13 Ways to Improve Emotional Intelligence at Home and at School

By
Deborah Fay

Copyright © 2017 Deborah Fay

First published 2017
by MJL Publications for My Juicy Life

    17 Spencer Avenue
    Moreton Downs, Deception Bay
    Queensland, Australia 4508
    Email: deb@debfay.com.au
    Phone: +61408735936
    Web: http://www.mjlpublications.com.au

All rights reserved. Without limiting the rights under copyright reserved above, no part of this publication may be reproduced, stored in or introduced in to a database and retrieval system, or transmitted in any form or by any means (electronic, mechanical, photocopying, recording or otherwise) without the prior written permission of both the owner of the copyright and the above publishers.

Grow Up

Fay, Deborah

ISBN: #978-0-648-37780-1

"The reasonable man adapts himself to the world: the unreasonable one persists in trying to adapt the world to himself. Therefore, all progress depends on the unreasonable man."

— George Bernard Shaw

Table of Contents

Introduction 9

My Story 13

Chapter 1 23

Understand the Five Stages of Emotional Intelligence .. 23

Chapter 2 31

Understand the Four Stages of Learning 31

Chapter 3 39

Reduce Your Child's Toxic Load 39

Chapter 4 47

Think Long Term 47

Chapter 5 53

Practice Relaxing 53

Chapter 6 59

Practice Checking In 59

Chapter 7 63

Pre-plan Your Responses to a Variety of Situations 63

Chapter 8 67

Manage Yourself First 67

Chapter 9 73

Broaden Your Experiences 73

Chapter 10 77

Learn to Communicate Feelings and Meet Needs Effectively *77*

Chapter 11 .... *83*

Make Good Choices for the Right Reasons *83*

Chapter 12 .... *87*

Review Everything *87*

Chapter 13 .... *91*

Model Forgiveness *91*

Final Words *95*

About Deborah Fay *99*

What Others Have Said About Deborah's Work *103*

Introduction

Grow Up – 13 Ways To Improve Emotional Intelligence at Home and at School has been written to help parents and teachers navigate what can only be described as the ever-colourful journey associated with raising and educating children.

It has been written specifically for parents and teachers who are sometimes, or often challenged by children who are at various stages of development and children who might be acting out and displaying any one or more of the following:

- Challenging behaviours
- Emotional outbursts
- Extreme emotions
- Obvious developmental delays or impairments
- Social development challenges
- Language issues
- Physical issues such as fine or gross motor delays
- Executive functioning issues
- Impulse control
- Inability to follow instructions
- Difficulty getting and staying on task

My intention in writing this book is to address some of these issues and bring a different understanding as well as a step-by-step guide to parents and teachers that will make life easier, more manageable and more enjoyable for parents, teachers *and* children.

Specifically, I intend to introduce you to the 5 stages of Emotional Intelligence model that I work from and give you an idea of the massive impact emotional intelligence has on all aspects of life.

You will also learn about the 4 Stages of Learning and be able to identify what stage a child is at in their learning of various skills which will in turn help you to know how you can encourage them to reach their developmental goals.

I will also teach you a process that I call the FERN Process, which is a simple step-by-step guide for managing and communicating emotions.

I have no doubt that any piece of information from this book that you come to understand and choose to implement into your parenting and teaching will have a significantly positive impact on your own life as well as your child or your student's life.

Above all, I encourage you to do your best to enjoy the process of consciously facilitating emotional intelligence. It is such a worthwhile endeavour.

My Story

I grew up in what I thought was a normal household. I went to a state primary school and I had the option to go to an all girls' high school which I jumped at because by the age of 12 I had come to the conclusion that boys were a bit annoying and I was a serious sort of kid.

It was with 20/20 hindsight, however, that I realised my household wasn't really normal. It was just normal for us. My father was away with the Army for most of my first 4 years, my mother was often unwell due to chronic lung issues resulting from mercury poisoning and my big brother was a little out of control which I suspect was a big part of the reason I'd decided boys were a bit annoying. The Psychiatrist told my mum that my brother was a "no" child and told her that she just had to learn to deal with him.

Further to that, I was often sick with allergies, asthma and kidney issues. I was an RH- baby so I'd had blood transfusions and lots of antibiotics as a baby, which I suspect set up an imbalance in my immunity. I didn't actually speak until I was 4½ (which in itself is a bit of a red flag) but could very well have been due to that imbalance. When I did start to speak I came out with whole sentences and I'd taught myself to read before I went to school.

I made it through high school and I tried a number of different jobs before I met my husband when we were in our early 20's. He was a little out of control when he was younger too and had also grown up in an interesting household with a different set of normal going on.

So, when our kids started arriving a few years later, we probably shouldn't have been surprised when we found out that our 1st child was being sent to the office during nap time at kindy so that they didn't disrupt the other kids. Nor should we have been surprised at the list of other conditions and behaviours that we now recognise as delays in executive functioning and common ADHD traits.

Our 2nd child was quieter and so much easier to manage, but we were worried that he was a little *too* withdrawn. He was diagnosed with Asperger's Syndrome at 7 after a range of red flags were raised at school about the way he was developing.

And our 3rd child seemed to develop quite normally until I weaned him from formula to cow's milk at 18 months and he stopped talking. It took us 12 months to realise the connection and we had quite a bit of work to do to undo the damage that was done developmentally. I expected he would be diagnosed with Autism Spectrum Disorder (ASD) when we found ourselves in a Paediatrician's office a few years later, but he was diagnosed with Generalised Anxiety Disorder (GAD) as an interim diagnosis and we were given the space to see if any ASD traits would remain once we were able to manage his anxiety.

There were 3 significant turning points for me as a mother that I wish to share here.

The first turning point happened just after our 2nd child was diagnosed with Asperger's. It was quite late at night and I recall feeling very alone and unsure about myself and my ability to be what my children needed me to be. I had absolutely no clue as to how I was going to parent my unique children, let alone do it adequately, and I felt I was failing them. I didn't understand why I'd been given these three beautiful innocent souls to care for when I was so unworthy. Then I heard the words, "No one person is worthy of the role of parent." and it gave me some peace. I understood that to mean that we have to *become* worthy of the role – we grow into it – and while some do better than others, and have better upbringings and role models than others, parenting is an opportunity for us to become who our children need us to become.

The second turning point for me came when we were sitting in the paediatrician's office waiting for a diagnosis of ASD for our 3rd child. I was very emotional through the appointment and when the doctor asked how we would feel about going with a diagnosis of GAD I mentioned to him that there was a lot of anxiety in my family. He looked me straight in the eye and said, "Yes I can see it," which had me baffled for a moment; but then it hit me that he was talking about me. It had never occurred to me before then that I might be experiencing the world through a heightened sensory state that accompanies fight or flight, and that things might not have been as big or as loud or as bright or as frightening as I had always thought they were.

The third and biggest turning point for me came shortly after that, just one week after my 1st child's 14th birthday. We found out that they had been cutting themself, and I was shattered. I didn't see it coming. They were always so bouncy and imaginative and on the go, so we couldn't see how deeply unhappy they were with themself and their life.

So, here we were, having made all of the biomedical changes and everything seemed to be on track, but now it was time to start working on our *emotional intelligence*.

Many years have passed since then. We have all done a lot of "personal development" and we continue to do so because, as it turns out, working on yourself is actually quite liberating and makes a positive difference to the way in which we experience and manage every other area of life.

We are not fixed or perfect or bullet proof yet, but we are happy and functional as a family unit and as individuals and we are well placed to manage ourselves in the face of a range of challenges should life choose to present them to us. I could not be happier with that.

Now, as a qualified counsellor, I am particularly passionate about teaching Emotional Intelligence and emotional resilience to people of all ages and apart from enjoying helping individuals to enjoy happier, healthier lives, I have no doubt that developing Emotional Intelligence or EQ is the answer to reducing incidences of relationship breakdowns, domestic violence, crime and suicide rates amongst other things. There is something very satisfying about being able to turn your challenges into wins and I feel certain that we have been able to do that in our family and will continue to do so as long as we are able.

Our children are with us

for a reason.

Our mission,

should we choose to accept it,

is to grow into our role

and become the parents

and teachers

they need us to be for them.

13 Ways to Improve Emotional Intelligence at Home and at School

Chapter 1
Understand the Five Stages of Emotional Intelligence

The 5 Stages of Emotional Intelligence model that I work from is an ever so slightly adapted version of the one presented to us by Daniel Goleman in the '90s. It is the model by which I gauge where a person is at in terms of their emotional maturity and it is enormously helpful in terms of being able to determine what sort of behaviour I can expect from someone and what I need to offer them to help them advance in their emotional maturity.

As parents, caregivers and teachers our ability to raise and adequately educate a child in the best of circumstances takes effort, but when you have a lot of children in your care and one or more are at the extreme outer edges of the range of maturity and development, it is very challenging.

By sharing the 5 Stages of Emotional Intelligence with you today, it is my intention that you will have a simple and basic model you can use to direct you in facilitating greater emotional literacy and greater emotional maturity.

I am talking about having a model that you can use like a step-by-step guide with every child in your care, regardless of where they are at in their development and regardless of what is happening for them.

Understand the Five Stages of Emotional Intelligence

The particular model I use is as follows:

1. **Self-Awareness**
2. **Self-Management**
3. **Social Awareness**
4. **Relationship Skills**
5. **Responsible Decision making**

1. Self-Awareness is simply the ability to identify and measure our feelings. Simple doesn't necessarily mean easy however so this is something that we need to practice a lot before we can become confident in our ability to judge and move forward most effectively.

In order to do this, we need practice at naming our feelings and it is not uncommon for families to have a limited emotional vocabulary.

A list of emotions is a great place to start. You could put one on the fridge at home or on the wall in the classroom and when a child is stuck in this phase he or she can always be directed to the chart to find the emotion that best fits what they are feeling in that moment.

Beside the list of emotions you could put a picture of a thermometer with a scale of 1-10 with one being at the bottom and 10 being at the top and you could ask your child to show you on the thermometer just how intense their feelings were.

Using a visual like a thermometer gives us a quick and effective reality check that tells us how soon we must act and with what level of our attention will be required.

The more experienced our children are at naming their emotions and identifying how intense they are, the easier they will find it to move to the next stage on the Emotional Intelligence model which is Self-Management.

2. Self-Management is simply the ability to manage ourselves in a variety of states and a variety of circumstances and there are many adults in this world who struggle with this so it is important that your expectations of your child or student is realistic so as not to add shame or doubt to the child's mind at this crucial stage in their learning.

The more accurate we can become in identifying and measuring our feelings, the more accurate we will become in identifying what our needs are and when we understand what our needs are, we are going to be more successful at meeting them.

It makes perfect sense then, that if we are struggling to regulate or manage our behaviour in a given situation, that we probably need to go back to stage one and ask ourselves once again to name our feelings and measure them. And we might need to do this a few times before we get this right but once we do, we will be able to identify what we need in order to be able to manage our behaviours or know who to ask for help in doing so.

Sometimes we miss the moment and the need to regulate turns into the need to soothe. We can use this model just as effectively to help a child identify what he or she needs in order to bounce back and feel happy again.

3. Social Awareness comes next and is simply our ability to understand the impact we have on the people around us.

There is a lot of talk about Theory of Mind in circles where Pervasive Development Disorders exist, which refers to a child's ability to perceive what another person might be feeling in a given situation.

This is considered a big part of the reason some children experience the social isolation they do but there is a way to grow social awareness, if it doesn't seem to come naturally to your child, and that is by broadening your child's experiences and then using the Emotional Intelligence model to help your child become consciously aware of their own feelings and their own needs in those settings.

If a child is reluctant to try new things or has high levels of anxiety you can use tools such as Carol Grey's Social Stories to help your child to become familiar with a variety of experiences without even leaving home or leaving the classroom. Any sort of visualisation exercise from the safety of a child's familiar environment is going to help them to stretch without traumatising a child, which could potentially take a child further from where they need to be.

4. Relationship Skills are next and learning these comes much easier when a child is adequately developing through the first three stages of the Emotional Intelligence model.

Being able to communicate effectively, work and play in teams, and reach outcomes that require the presence of others is vital for a healthy, whole individual in our society.

Once again, if a child is being challenged in this area, go back to stage one and ask the questions, what are you feeling and how intense are your feelings.

Move then to stage two and ask the child what they need to be able to self-regulate or self-soothe, and once that is under control find out if the child needs exposure to a different experience or to do some visualisation to be able to work through the relationship issue that has presented itself.

For communication issues the FERN Process will be helpful here. This is a process I developed to help myself, and others, to process through difficult emotions and communicate them effectively to other people. I will talk about this later in the book but in short it is a process of questions that incorporates the first three stages of emotional intelligence and gives us a script to use to communicate our needs to others in a way that others can make sense of.

5. Responsible Decision-Making is the final stage and when you are raising or teaching a child that is impulsive, sensitive and

Understand the Five Stages of Emotional Intelligence

doesn't think things through, responsible decision-making skills sounds like a dream.

The fact of the matter however is that when anyone, let alone a child can articulate their feelings, adequately measure the intensity of them, be able to identify their need and fill it using healthy and effective communication skills then they are capable of being response-able and of thinking things through so that they can come up with a responsible decision.

It is a lack of positive experience in the first four stages of Emotional Intelligence that cause a person to be reactive, which often takes that person from one bad experience to another to another.

Knowing yourself, knowing how to manage yourself, knowing how you are impacting on the people around you and knowing how to communicate effectively with them will automatically help you to make more response-able decisions.

Emotional Intelligence is *knowing that you know* these things.

Chapter 2
Understand the Four Stages of Learning

The Four Stages of Learning, also known as the Four Stages of Competency explains the stages we go through whenever we are learning a new skill or a new set of skills.

1 Unconscious Incompetent	2 Conscious Incompetent
3 Conscious Competent	4 Unconscious Competent

Understand the Four Stages of Learning

This model reflects the essence of neural development and the building of networks in the brain and like the Five Stages of Emotional Intelligence, I find this a particularly useful tool for identifying where a child is at in their development and what can be expected in terms of their behaviour at that particular time.

The four stages shown in the figure above identify our level of consciousness during various states of competency and are more about our awareness of ourselves during learning than they are about the learning itself, but when we understand ourselves in relation to these stages we can move through them with greater ease and confidence and know we are on the right track regardless of how uncomfortable we might be feeling at any particular stage.

In stage one we basically have no clue that we have no clue. We are unaware that we are unaware. Some people might refer to this stage as ignorant bliss but it is my experience that there are very few occasions in life when ignorance is actually helpful and in fact, more often than not, the longer one remains in ignorance, the more damage can be done that will ultimately need to be undone.

An example of unconscious incompetent would be when we are first born and we only have awareness around our immediate environment. We have neither the need nor the desire to turn a computer on or drive a car.

Stage two is when we become aware that we have no clue. The six-year-old child that sees another six-year-old on a bmx bicycle having the time of his life is suddenly driven to have that experience for himself and no matter how hard he tries to recreate what he saw his buddy doing, he can't yet make it happen for himself. He is now very aware that there is something he doesn't know which puts him into the conscious incompetent stage of learning.

Stage three is where all the action happens. This is where neural networks are built and where life opens up to us. But it is also the stage where we are most uncomfortable and where our character is developed.

Conscious Competent is the stage in which we learn a new skill. Learning to ride the pushbike is a good example of this stage because we are required to give a great deal of our conscious attention to the task in order to complete it. Learning to drive a car is quite complicated and requires even more conscious attention.

It is often particularly uncomfortable to be in this space and the reason for that is because we are building some neural pathways for the very first time. We might be building upon networks that already exist but we are still performing brand new tasks that require brand new pathways.

This is the stage in which artists and creative personalities spend most of their time while they create amazing works of art, music or written masterpieces.

Understand the Four Stages of Learning

It is the stage where neural development occurs. Each time we perform a new task the new pathway is myelinated or coated in essential fatty acids, hence the need for fish oil in our diet.

The more we perform the task the more the pathway is coated and the quicker the electrical impulses move along the pathway, until eventually there is seemingly little or no time between the decision to act and the action itself.

Which brings us to the fourth stage of learning. Unconscious Competent is the stage where we know how to perform a task or set of tasks so well that we no longer have to think about it at all. It seems to happen automatically and effortlessly. We have officially mastered it.

The saying *practice makes perfect* is appropriate here although it is more likely *perfect practice makes perfect* because if you practice something incorrectly then you are going to master it incorrectly. Just something to consider while you are in the Conscious Competent stage of learning.

The other important thing to note here is that going through the Conscious Competent stage is the perfect time to be practicing the Five Stages of Emotional Intelligence. If a child can learn to be self-aware, self-manage, be socially aware and practice relationship skills through this stage then he or she will move through the Conscious Competent stage more efficiently and as a result he or she will have mastered the Four Stages of Learning. That means he knows he has the ability to master anything he sets his mind to and that really is something worth mastering in my opinion.

Until then, as long as we understand the Four Stages of Learning we can determine where our children or students are and actively direct and encourage them toward mastering the task or set of tasks in front of them.

Breaking a task into smaller tasks is helpful because it minimises the discomfort of the conscious competent stage and with every smaller task mastered there is the opportunity for building self-esteem as the child sees him or herself achieving the goals set out.

Have a big carrot is helpful to all of us when we are learning something new and celebrating every win is helpful to reinforce future efforts.

All of these things help set our children up to win and as long as we include them in the process they will know how to do this for themselves.

Chapter 3
Reduce Your Child's Toxic Load

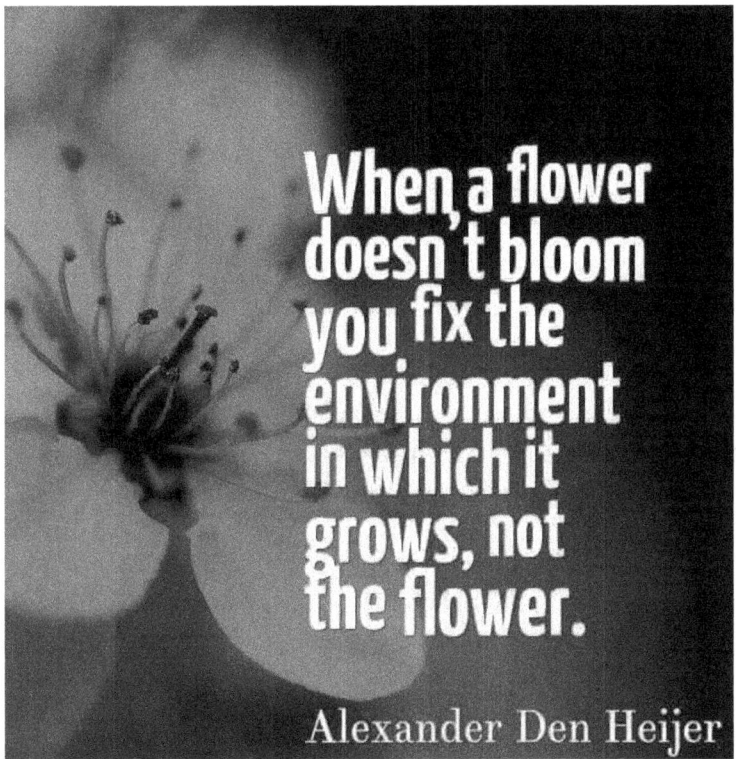

In the same way that a plant needs a certain environment in which to thrive, so does a child. A child cannot thrive in a toxic environment whether that is his home, his family, his school or his body.

Please do not underestimate the role of stress on the body and please do not underestimate the role of immunity in development.

We personally had to learn a lot about this and great strides were made in development by addressing toxic load.

According to Dr Gary Deed, our bodies are either in an anabolic or catabolic state – building up or breaking down – and my understanding is that when our toxic load is high the body's resources are constantly being redirected away from development toward managing that load. It is the squeakiest wheel and if it is never adequately addressed then development suffers.

We have to try to ensure that nothing gets in the way of healthy development so that our children have the best possible chance of becoming strong and healthy and smart and successful.

Think of toxins as having two manageable sources – emotional and chemical – both of which have a negative psychological and physical impact on the body.

Living in an environment where there is constant emotional conflict, fear, drama and no clear boundaries will place a child into a fight or flight mode more often than is healthy.

Harassment or bullying or pushing a child beyond the threshold of what they can tolerate has the same affect and any unused adrenalin and cortisol becomes toxic and places a load onto a child's body.

We need to ensure that a child feels safe and has his basic needs met in order to be psychologically sound and working on building emotional intelligence via the Five Stages of Emotional Intelligence is a great way to go to achieve this.

Synthetic substances in our environment make up the chemical source of toxins that add to a child's toxic load and while this might seem like an endless source, every little thing we do to reduce this load is helpful.

Here are six ideas of places where you can start to reduce your child's exposure to any synthetic substances that might be adding to his or her toxic load and drawing constantly on his immune system.

1 Perfumes – Stop using perfumes and replace any products with perfume or scent in them. Swap them out for products that are organic unscented or scented with essential oils. Not only will that reduce the load, but depending on what oils you use and how you use them, you might even be supporting your child's immune system.

I strongly urge parents to discourage teens from using the strongly scented underarm and body sprays that are marketed to them. I especially urge you to discourage them from spraying them liberally in a closed space. There are so many synthetic and potentially harmful chemicals in these products.

2. MSG – any products with savoury flavouring will likely have MSG in it and any products with numbers in the 600 ranges are to be avoided. Products such as chips and biscuits and 2-minute noodles and soups are likely laden with MSG and the less of this the better.

3. Pesticides – they are poisonous so stop spraying and start using baits and natural deterrents instead. These things might

be tolerable on their own but in conjunction with all the other synthetic products we are exposed to might be make them the tipping point and the difference between a healthy or an unhealthy child.

4. Where possible use natural products and avoid petrochemicals such as sodium laurel sulphates and propylene glycol. It is not difficult to make your own basic cleaning products using very basic ingredients and including essential oils. Nor is it difficult to swap out many personal care products for natural alternatives. You would be amazed what a jar of organic coconut oil and a good essential oil can do for you.

5. Swap out plastic storage for glass where possible.

6. Test for food intolerances and allergies and do an elimination of those things that you might not have been aware were causing digestive issues for your child. For example, gluten might not have an immediate impact on your child's behaviour but it might be getting in the way of the digestion of the essential fatty acids in the diet that are required for the myelination process that happens during neural development.

You will find a good professional that specialises in this area will be helpful if you are serious about addressing it and there are so many more places to go with this step but to reiterate what I said earlier, every step you take and every thing you do to reduce the toxic load is going to help.

We sought support from a GP who had the additional qualifications in nutritional and environmental medicine.

An integrative doctor will be able to help you, and a GAPS certified practitioner would also be able to help.

Here is a direct link where you can hopefully find an integrative doctor near you:

http://www.biobalance.org.au/patients

Thankfully more and more professionals are specialising in this area of health so there are more choices for us as parents than ever before.

As teachers there are some areas here where you can have an impact, including maintaining a chemically safe classroom through to helping to educate children and their families about healthier choices that will help enhance the learning process.

Chapter 4
Think Long Term

What goals do you have for your child or student?

It can be so easy to get caught up in a challenging moment and even lose sight of where we want to go when we are being tested and our tolerance levels are low.

I always thought I would like my children to grow up to become confident, caring and cooperative human beings and I believe we have achieved that, but that was as far as I had thought in terms of setting goals for them.

Now I realise that having short, medium and long-term goals for your children is very important for a number of valid reasons.

Teachers have year-long academic goals of course but how lovely it would be to have parents and teachers contributing to the same bigger picture while working on the short and medium-term goals in academics and social emotional learning.

As I have said, there are some very good reasons to have long-term goals and this is especially true when you have a child that has some developmental or behavioural issues.

Holding a broader vision for your child or student, however, can help you to rise above what is happening in any particular moment and can help you to navigate a discussion or interaction toward a higher purpose and away from what might have been a control issue or debate about right or wrong.

Motivational speaker Tony Robbins once explained that a racing car driver who is about to crash is trained to literally turn his heads toward where he wants to go and away from where he thinks he is heading.

This is sort of what we need to do as adults when our engagement with a child is about to crash and burn. We need to turn our heads toward the bigger picture and focus on where we want to go so that we can lead our children in that direction and get them focused on where everyone needs to be for the greater good.

I believe our job as parents and teachers is to teach and foster independence so being able to model this approach is invaluable.

Including a child in the goal-setting process is also helpful on many levels. Apart from teaching them to set goals and think long term, it gives them the broader vision and helps them to rise above on their own.

We all have ideas about what is right and wrong, where we should or shouldn't be and what we should or shouldn't be doing at any given time, but having a broader, long term vision can help us to let go of any ideas that don't fit that vision giving us more energy and attention to bring to the moment.

Finally, thinking long term can take unnecessary pressure off the present moment and help us to stay focused on what really matters and what needs our attention most.

I also believe it is better to work on one goal at a time and a long-term vision will make it easier to prioritise what that goal needs to be in the present.

Chapter 5
Practice Relaxing

Whether parent, caregiver or teacher, I urge you to make time to practice relaxing with your child or student. It is very important to practice it on a regular basis and only contributes positively to a healthier more tolerant disposition.

Practicing relaxing is important for returning little and big bodies to the relaxed pose or the opposite of the fight and flight state.

Practicing relaxing increases physical and emotional tolerance levels and makes us more resilient on many levels.

Practicing relaxing improves our digestion and the absorption of nutrients, which help with development and also help to improve our tolerance levels.

Practice Relaxing

Practicing relaxing helps us to observe and experience things as they are and not from a hyper-vigilant state of fight or flight where things are louder, brighter and more intense for us than they are in reality.

Practicing relaxing builds neural pathways in our brain that help us to manage impulsivity and reactivity.

A daily meditation practice is the best way to practice relaxing and learning to be still is a skill that will benefit every area of life and give us the ability to respond rather than react to what life is presenting to us.

Resistance to meditation is very common until we have moved through the conscious competent stage and have mastered the habit. Until then it feels like work and can take a while to really be still.

Showing up daily to practice meditating is the first step to creating a lifelong habit and even if you start with 60 seconds of stillness you can grow your practice over time to benefit from longer periods of stillness.

When Buddha was asked: What have you gained from meditation? He said: Nothing but let me tell you what I have lost: anger, anxiety, depression, insecurity, fear of old age and death.

As a Counsellor, if I could only choose one tool to pass onto each of my clients to help them in their lives, I would choose meditation.

You don't have to sit cross-legged and hold your fingers in any particular place. There are just 4 things you need to do:

1. Find or create a space that you can easily go to every day where you won't be disturbed and where you will be inspired to get in to a still space within (this can be a fun, creative exercise within itself),

2. Show up every day (very important),

3. Sit comfortably with you back straight, then

4. Inhale, exhale and repeat for up to 20 minutes.

I encourage you to commit to the process and find out for yourself how powerful it is for you, and for your child's emotional development.

Chapter 6
Practice Checking In

Grow Up

Checking in builds self-awareness. There is a great deal of value in randomly asking ourselves how we are feeling in any moment and the same goes for our children.

If we practice checking in randomly instead of waiting for a drama or incident to occur then chances are that the child will find it easier to articulate their feelings and measure them when they are under pressure or when their feelings are heightened.

1. Very simply, whenever the thought occurs to you, ask a child to name how they are feeling in that moment. You might allow them to offer up to three emotions to help build emotional literacy.

2. Then ask them to describe the intensity of their feelings

3. Finally, ask them to identify any needs they might have in that moment.

Once again, you are building neural pathways when you start to practice this so it might take a while to carry out this exercise to begin with but over time it will become automatic and be much quicker.

I get so excited to think of a future where all parents and teachers do this automatically and we are able to raise a whole generation of emotionally confident children. It is possible.

Chapter 7
Pre-plan Your Responses to a Variety of Situations

Taking time to create a plan of attack is a great way to deal with a variety of situations and improve emotional intelligence.

Get proactive. What *might* happen today, tomorrow, next week or at a particular event? You can literally use visualisation to build neural pathways in advance.

The very act of discussing experiences and options is so helpful when something new is coming up for one of your children or when the class is embarking on a new project or learning trajectory.

It is also really helpful when a child is having a difficult time with a challenging situation and can't seem to find adequate solutions.

Parents can use the dinner table to discuss explore options and pre-plan responses to various situations, thereby helping a child to feel more confident when they are facing the situation that is so challenging for them.

Teachers might use floor time to do the same and allow the children to brainstorm and work together to problem solve. No doubt other children will have similar experiences and will benefit from exploring one child's challenges.

It's not difficult to see how having a plan of attack can help a child respond with more confidences and be more prepared to handle things better emotionally.

One of the biggest challenges to doing this enough is going to be time because we are all challenged in this area but preparing

Pre-plan Your Responses to a Variety of Situations

our children and helping them to be independent will save time in the long run because we won't be consistently putting out fires with them or for them.

Chapter 8
Manage Yourself First

Because of the nature of learning and neural development, children learn by imitating us. They see us doing something and unconsciously act as they have seen us acting.

It can be quite humbling at times to see a child acting out in response to something. Hearing your words coming out of their mouths or seeing them acting as you have acted can be quite confronting and you might find yourself wanting to act out in anger or frustration yourself.

If you can't manage yourself first, you are going to find it difficult to teach your child or student to manage their self.

Throwing a wobbly or a tantrum is not just reserved for the terrible twos. Have a think about that for a moment. What does a wobbly look like and sound like? It sounds like someone getting loud and boisterous and angry and intimidating and flustered and it looks like someone throwing their arms around and pointing fingers and slamming doors and windows and possibly even throwing things around. Sometimes it goes so far as to look like someone throwing punches or kicks.

Regardless of who or what triggered such a response, or hold old you are, a tantrum is a tantrum and it is not the result of someone who is managing themselves or their feelings.

I know putting a child into time out has always been considered an appropriate tool for parents and teachers to use to help a child to calm their emotions or consider their actions in a still and quiet environment.

I also know a number of parents and some teachers who would benefit from time out. Myself included.

Has your behaviour always been "grown up"?

Have your responses to your children, your partner, your friends, your family or your work colleagues always been "managed" appropriately?

Do you still struggle now to manage your own emotions when you feel pushed or cornered or triggered by something or someone?

If you are honest, then the answer to that last question has to be yes. Yet some of us expect children to be perfect and we are not happy when they are not.

I encourage you to put the learning in this book into practice in your own life and build your own emotional intelligence first. From my own experience, when I changed my own focus from parenting and teaching my children to parenting and teaching myself, a little bit of magic happened and my children started growing up.

It seems they just needed me to show them rather than tell them how.

Here are some things you can do to manage yourself first:

- Practice relaxing to keep your tolerance levels high
- Practice checking in so you can self-regulate or self-soothe
- Don't be afraid to take time out for yourself
- Model what it looks like to identify and take care of your needs before they get too big to manage
- Be the change you want to see in your children
- Ask yourself, am I managing myself adequately?

Chapter 9
Broaden Your Experiences

When I described the development of Social Awareness I briefly explained how broadening our experiences and using the first two stages of the emotional intelligence model could help us to further develop our ability to imagine how someone else might be feeling in a particular situation. It also could help us to imagine the type of impact our words and behaviours might be having on the people around us, which is vital for building relationships, but there are so many more advantages to doing this.

Presenting our children with a broad range of experiences is a great way to develop emotional literacy, emotional confidence and emotional intelligence.

Because of my own fears and anxieties I was always willing to avoid new experiences or avoid encouraging my kids to participate in new things, but I know now that we did ourselves a disservice.

Past studies have revealed that up to 1 in 5 babies will naturally have a more heightened fight or flight response to a perceived threat, and those same babies will take a much longer time to recover and return to the relaxed response.

By the time children are at school up to 1 in 10 children still have a similar response to a perceived threat and so it is considered that up to 10% of the population is prone to anxiety.

Of course, there is not only one degree or intensity of feeling when we are talking about anxiety. There are many different degrees or intensities of the same feelings, and there are many children who have a variety of experiences of anxiety.

Those children might require additional support when stepping out of their comfort zones and they might resist with all they've got, but that does not mean they don't need to have new experiences. In fact, it might mean they need new experiences more than other children their age.

We need to set up some experiences differently or put scaffolding in place to help them experience new things in a way that is safe and supportive and enjoyable.

Then we use the Five Stages of Emotional Intelligence to build self-awareness and to self-manage during and after the experience.

Going through the new experience will require us all to be in the uncomfortable state of conscious competent but the first time is always the hardest if it is set up correctly and you have pre-planned the event so that everyone has a successful event.

Remember to check in constantly when you are doing new things with a child to be sure they are where you want them to be emotionally.

Chapter 10
Learn to Communicate Feelings and Meet Needs Effectively

One of the most effective tools I use myself as well as teach to others to help them process through difficult emotions is a tool I call the FERN Process.

The process is for anyone who has challenging emotions, which we all do at times, and it can take a person very quickly from feeling completely lost or out of control to a place where they can clearly articulate what they need with confidence and calm.

It is a four-question process that helps us to separate the facts from our fears, helps us identify and measure our emotional response to a situation, and then helps us to identify what it is we need in order to move forward.

It is a perfect way to put the Five Stages of Emotional Intelligence into practice building self-awareness, self-management skills and social awareness skills, and is a wonderful tool relationship skill in itself as it is a tool for communicating boundaries and needs with others.

FERN is an acronym and stands for the following:

F = Fact / Fiction
E = Emotional
R = Response
N = Need

The FERN Process is not only a way to understand ourselves better and work out what we need, it is also a script we can use when we need to set boundaries with someone else or when we need to ask for support from someone.

Learn to Communicate Feelings and Meet Needs Effectively

The process goes as follows:

FACT = What happened?
It is important to stick strictly to the facts here.

FICTION = What am I telling myself might be happening?

This is where we let our minds run ahead of us so what story we are telling ourselves about what is going on or why someone might be acting as they are.

Much of the time we are having an emotional response to the fiction we are buying into than we are to the facts so learning to separate the two is vital for building emotional intelligence.

EMOTIONAL RESPONSE = What am I feeling?

It is important to name the feeling and become aware of whether the feelings relate to the fact or the fiction.

NEED = What do I need now so that I can move forward?

When you correctly identify the emotion you are feeling it will be reasonably easy to figure out what you need.

You might need to set a boundary with someone, you might need to stick up for yourself, you might need to ask for help, you might need to eat or have a bath or sleep.

Many people are able to tell us how they feel but then they get stuck in their feelings and often feel like they are going around and around in circles.

Asking ourselves what we need is the key to moving on and if we don't adequately identify and name the emotions we are feeling we might need to go back over the process until we get closer to the truth. There is no right or wrong answer here. There is just what you feel and then what you need in order to make things right.

Finally, you can use the FERN Process as a script when you need to speak up for yourself, make someone aware of how you want to be treated, set a boundary with someone or ask for help in meeting a need.

You can literally read it word for word off your journal and it will give the person you are addressing a clear and calm picture of what is happening for you and what you need from them.

To be sure they have heard you correctly and have understood the message you are trying to convey to them, simply ask them:

What did you hear me say?

When they repeat back to you what they heard you will be able to gage whether or not they received your message correctly or if you need to explain further.

Using the FERN Process is definitely uncomfortable for many to begin with because it is a completely new way to process through information and feelings.

Use a journal and write the process out to begin with and just remember that you are in the Conscious Competent stage as you are building new networks in your brain.

Learn to Communicate Feelings and Meet Needs Effectively

Before long this way of processing will be perfectly natural for you and you won't have to write it down as much. You will be able to run through the questions in your mind in the heat of an emotionally charged moment and you will know exactly how you feel, what you need, and how to express yourself calmly and confidently.

The FERN Process is a remarkable tool for improving emotional literacy, emotional confidence and emotional intelligence so I encourage you to persist through the Conscious Competent stage and master the skill.

Chapter 11
Make Good Choices for the Right Reasons

Something that I think we seem to have lost sight of in today's society is the ability to make good choices for the right reasons.

There seems to be an enormous focus on how we feel about everything and we aren't necessarily making the best choices for ourselves because we don't want to feel bad or feel stressed or feel uncomfortable.

This is often the result of having had parents who love us so much that they are even willing to save us from the consequences of our own actions, thereby stopping us from fully understanding how we impact on the world and how the world responds to certain behaviours.

Emotional intelligence teaches us how to manage ourselves in the face of challenges and hardship. We might not always feel like doing something but some things are good for us regardless of how we feel about it.

Here are some reasons why we might choose to do something uncomfortable or even painful:

- It's good for me
- It's in line with my goals and values
- It's the right thing to do
- It's in my best interest

Helping children to understand this is very important but allowing them to experience it for themselves is the most important thing you can do for them.

Make Good Choices for the Right Reasons

Let them experience the natural consequences of their actions. Let them experience some pain and hardship and discomfort and use the Five Stages of Emotional Intelligence to help them work through their discomfort but do not save them.

Once they are through the other side and have survived making the right choices for the right reasons then don't be afraid to celebrate and reward to reinforce the behaviour but don't use a reward as a carrot.

A big part of Emotional Intelligence is knowing that we are capable of making good choices for the right reasons.

Chapter 12
Review Everything

Step 7 suggests we pre-plan and prepare our children and for the future, to get proactive and to consider what *might* happen today, tomorrow, next week or at a particular event?

Step 12 is about looking back over events so that we can learn as much as possible and set ourselves up to be better and do better should a similar situation arise in the future.

Whether we are reviewing a period of time or a particular event, asking the following questions will help us build self-awareness, social awareness and relationships skills for future events. It will also help us consider better ways to self-manage.

You could be reviewing a day at school, an excursion, a play date or family outing.

What worked?
What did I do well?
What didn't work?
What could I have done better?
How can we set it up or make it better next time?
How can I be better next time?

It is important to look for positives as well as opportunities to improve so that our experiences of life are more to our liking and we can grow into emotionally confident beings who can bounce back positively from lots of different situations.

Chapter 13
Model Forgiveness

The final step to improving emotional intelligence at home and at school is to model forgiveness.

We all make mistakes. Being human is a ongoing process of learning and teaching and growing and loving and losing and falling and getting back up and starting over.

Forgive yourself and let your children and students see you doing that. Dust yourself off then go back and do it all again with courage, confidence and conviction.

Please, please, *please* do not punish yourself for not having all the answers.

Practice (and model) self-compassion for your children.

Please, please, please do not punish a child for not having the learning or development you think they should have at any given time.

Understand the difference between natural consequences and punishment. Natural consequences are not laden with heavy emotion. They just are what they are and they teach us everything we need to learn.

Punishment on the other hand promotes feelings of shame and disgust and other negative emotions that can keep a child emotionally stunted.

Allow natural consequences. Keep learning and keep teaching and keep loving.

Final Words

Know that we cannot teach what we do not know and it is through our actions, not our words that we have the biggest impact, so we **must** practice what we preach.

"You must be the change you want to see in the world."
~ *Mahatma Gandhi*

Involve your children or students in the process of *your* learning and practicing emotional intelligence so that you grow together.

If everyone is learning and moving toward the same goal of emotional intelligence then there is no need to concern ourselves with control, just staying on task and it is better when we are helping each other.

About Deborah Fay

Grow Up

Deborah Fay is a Holistic Counsellor and Author who specialises in the understanding and practical application of Emotional Intelligence particularly in relation to building emotional resilience.

Deborah is a qualified Pathways to Resilience Facilitator for Teenagers and Pre-Teens, A Certified Member of the International Institute for Complimentary Therapists, a member of the International Meditation Teacher's Association and the Principal of My Juicy Life Counselling Services situated north of Brisbane.

About Deborah Fay

Deborah is passionate about emotional intelligence, relationships, social emotional learning and childhood development.

Other books by Deborah include:

Grow Up

6 Keys to Happiness

Domestic Detox

Parenting A Child on The Spectrum

The Value of Meditation

You can find all of Deborah's Books at www.mjlpubications.com.au

You can read Deborah's blog and access her services at www.debfay.com.au

What Others Have Said About Deborah's Work

Grow Up

*"It was nice to meet you on the weekend and I loved listening to your presentation, so interesting and engaging!!
I have already read your e-book [Grow Up] and the 6 Keys to Happiness book and they are amazing! I read lots of personal development books and your 2 books have been some of the most useful books I have read as they are simple, practical and contain really useful strategies."*

~ Beatrice Peters
Holistic Health Coach and Physiotherapist
www.beatricepeters.com.au

*"I LOVE YOUR BOOK [6 Keys to Happiness]!
I especially love the "worksheets" and blanks to complete. I believe it is useful to address these important questions about ourselves.
I have just placed an order for two [more] copies to give to two relatives whom I believe will resonate with the ideas that you write in your amazing book!"*

~ Dr Siti Hawa
Author and Speaker
www.drsitihawa.com

"I fully support the project [Parenting A Child On The Spectrum] and the concept of parents coming together to help other parents. It is a great idea and it's wonderful to see parents working together to create a book that brings help and hope to other parents."

What Others Have Said About Deborah's Work

~ Dr Renae Beaumont
Author and Creator of the Secret Agents Society
Head of Practitioner Training and Support at the Social Skills Training Institute and an Honorary Research Fellow at the University of Queensland
www.sst-institute.net

Grow Up

www.ingramcontent.com/pod-product-compliance
Lightning Source LLC
Chambersburg PA
CBHW071721040426
42446CB00011B/2155